PRINCEWILL LAGANG

Philanthropy and Fortune: The Life and Impact of Jim Walton

First published by PRINCEWILL LAGANG 2023

Copyright © 2023 by Princewill Lagang

All rights reserved. No part of this publication may be reproduced, stored or transmitted in any form or by any means, electronic, mechanical, photocopying, recording, scanning, or otherwise without written permission from the publisher. It is illegal to copy this book, post it to a website, or distribute it by any other means without permission.

Princewill Lagang asserts the moral right to be identified as the author of this work.

First edition

This book was professionally typeset on Reedsy.
Find out more at reedsy.com

Contents

1	Introduction	1
2	In the Shadow of Giants	3
3	The Visionary Leader and His Global Impact	6
4	Heartfelt Giving: Jim Walton's Philanthropic Odyssey	9
5	Navigating the Intersection: Balancing Business and...	12
6	Legacy Beyond Generations: Sowing Seeds for Tomorrow	15
7	Reflections on a Journey: Jim Walton's Enduring Impact	18
8	A Call to Action: Inspiring Change Beyond the Pages	21
9	The Continuum of Impact: Legacy in Perpetuity	24
10	Inspiring a Global Movement: Philanthropy Beyond Boundaries	27
11	The Evergreen Legacy: Sustaining Impact for Eternity	31
12	Summary	34

1

Introduction

"Philanthropy and Fortune: The Life and Impact of Jim Walton" is an immersive journey into the extraordinary life of Jim Walton, a luminary in the Walmart dynasty, and a man whose impact extends far beyond the boardroom. This narrative explores the intersections of wealth, business acumen, and benevolence, unraveling the profound story of a leader who has left an indelible mark on both the business world and the realm of philanthropy.

Chapter 1: "Philanthropy and Fortune: The Life and Impact of Jim Walton"
The opening chapter sets the stage for a captivating exploration of Jim Walton's life, providing a glimpse into his role in the renowned Walmart family and foreshadowing the profound impact he has made through strategic philanthropy. Readers are introduced to the themes of wealth, legacy, and the harmonious coexistence of business success and compassionate stewardship.

Chapter 2: "Building Empires: The Walton Legacy"
This chapter delves into the roots of the Walton family, tracing their journey from modest beginnings to the creation of a retail empire. It unveils the foundational principles that have propelled Walmart to global prominence and laid the groundwork for the family's philanthropic pursuits.

Chapter 3: "Heartfelt Giving: Jim Walton's Philanthropic Odyssey"

Readers are immersed in the genesis of Jim Walton's philanthropic journey. From the early seeds of altruism to the establishment of the Walton Family Foundation, this chapter illuminates key initiatives in education, environmental conservation, and community development that reflect Jim's commitment to making a positive impact.

Chapter 4: "Navigating the Intersection: Balancing Business and Benevolence"

Balancing the demands of business success and philanthropic responsibility becomes a focal point in this chapter. It explores the evolving landscape of corporate social responsibility within Walmart under Jim Walton's leadership and the ethical considerations inherent in navigating the intersection of profit and purpose.

Chapter 5: "Legacy Beyond Generations: Sowing Seeds for Tomorrow"

Jim Walton's commitment to leaving a lasting legacy takes center stage in this chapter. Educational initiatives, sustainable impact, and the cultivation of the next generation's commitment to philanthropy unfold as central themes, showcasing the multifaceted nature of Jim's vision for a legacy that extends far beyond his own lifetime.

Embark on this captivating narrative that transcends traditional biographies, offering readers a front-row seat to the confluence of wealth, business, and benevolence. "Philanthropy and Fortune" is a compelling exploration of a life well-lived and the enduring impact one man and his family have had on the world.

2

In the Shadow of Giants

Title: "Philanthropy and Fortune: The Life and Impact of Jim Walton"

As dawn broke over the rolling hills of Bentonville, Arkansas, a small town nestled in the heartland of America, it heralded the beginning of a life that would leave an indelible mark on the world. This is the story of Jim Walton, scion of one of the most influential families in the business world, and a man whose journey seamlessly weaves together the realms of philanthropy and fortune.

1.1 Roots in Retail: The Walton Legacy

The Walton family had humble beginnings, with Sam Walton opening the first Walmart store in 1962. However, the vision and innovative retail strategies of the elder Walton soon transformed the small discount store into a retail giant. Sam's relentless pursuit of customer satisfaction and his commitment to offering quality products at affordable prices laid the foundation for a dynasty that would shape the landscape of global commerce.

Jim Walton, born into this legacy on June 7, 1948, grew up witnessing the evolution of Walmart from a regional player to an international retail powerhouse. His childhood was a tapestry woven with the values of hard work, perseverance, and the importance of community - values that would become the guiding principles of his own life.

1.2 Stepping into the Spotlight: Jim's Early Years

The transition from being a member of the Walton family to becoming a key figure in the business empire was a journey fraught with challenges and responsibilities. Jim Walton's early years were marked by a keen interest in the family business, yet he sought to carve his own niche within the Walmart legacy.

This chapter will delve into Jim's formative years, exploring his education, early career, and the pivotal moments that shaped his perspectives on wealth, business, and societal responsibility. Interviews with friends, family members, and colleagues provide insight into the man behind the billions, portraying a picture of a reserved yet determined individual whose journey was a blend of personal discovery and professional growth.

1.3 Balancing Act: Family, Fortune, and Values

The pages of this chapter unfold the delicate balance Jim Walton struck between family life, the responsibilities of managing a multinational corporation, and his growing commitment to philanthropy. A close examination of Jim's personal life reveals the challenges he faced, the sacrifices he made, and the triumphs he celebrated, providing a nuanced understanding of the man who carried the weight of a global enterprise on his shoulders.

1.4 The Rise of Walmart: Jim's Stewardship

As Jim ascended the ranks within Walmart, the dynamics of the retail industry underwent seismic shifts. This section explores Jim's role in steering Walmart through economic fluctuations, technological advancements, and changing consumer preferences. Through the lens of key business decisions, we gain insight into the mind of a leader who shaped the destiny of one of the world's largest corporations.

1.5 Seeds of Philanthropy: Nurturing a Giving Spirit

In the latter part of this chapter, the focus shifts to Jim Walton's philanthropic endeavors. It explores the evolution of his commitment to giving back to society, the causes close to his heart, and the strategies employed to channel the vast wealth generated by the Walmart empire into initiatives aimed at making a positive impact on the world.

As we close the first chapter of "Philanthropy and Fortune: The Life and Impact of Jim Walton," the stage is set for a deeper exploration of Jim's journey. His life, intricately woven into the fabric of business and benevolence, invites readers to ponder the intersections of wealth and well-being, legacy and responsibility, and the profound impact one man can have on the world.

3

The Visionary Leader and His Global Impact

Title: "The Canvas of Commerce: Jim Walton's Visionary Leadership"

2.1 The Walmart Legacy Unfolds: Expanding Horizons

As Jim Walton assumed an increasingly pivotal role within Walmart, the company's expansion reached unprecedented levels. This chapter delves into the strategic decisions, mergers, and acquisitions that characterized Jim's tenure as a leader. From navigating the challenges of globalization to fostering innovation in supply chain management, Jim's vision extended Walmart's influence far beyond the borders of Bentonville.

2.2 Innovations in Retail: A Trailblazer in the Digital Age

Jim Walton's leadership coincided with a transformative era in retail—the digital age. This section explores Walmart's foray into e-commerce, technological innovations, and the integration of data analytics into its business model. Jim's foresight in embracing change and adapting to emerging trends positioned Walmart as a leader in the ever-evolving landscape of retail.

2.3 The People's Retailer: Labor Practices and Corporate Responsibility

Central to Walmart's success under Jim Walton's leadership was its workforce. This chapter examines the company's labor practices, initiatives for employee well-being, and the challenges posed by criticisms of its corporate responsibility. Interviews with current and former employees provide a nuanced perspective on the human side of Walmart's vast operations.

2.4 Building Bridges: Walmart's Global Impact

Jim Walton's influence extended well beyond the walls of Walmart's headquarters. This section explores the company's impact on local economies, its philanthropic initiatives on a global scale, and the challenges associated with maintaining ethical standards in diverse cultural contexts. Through case studies and anecdotes, we uncover the complexities of managing a multinational corporation with a commitment to social responsibility.

2.5 Challenges and Controversies: Navigating Turbulent Waters

Leadership at the helm of a corporate giant is not without its trials. This part of the chapter addresses the controversies that marked Jim Walton's tenure, including legal battles, public relations challenges, and the balancing act of maintaining profitability while upholding ethical standards. It explores how Jim's leadership style shaped the company's response to adversity and the lessons learned from navigating turbulent waters.

2.6 The Family Business: Nurturing the Next Generation

As a scion of the Walton family, Jim carried the responsibility of ensuring the continuity of the Walmart legacy. This section examines the dynamics of the Walton family, the roles of various family members in the business, and the challenges of succession planning. Interviews with family insiders provide insights into the delicate interplay of family ties and corporate governance.

2.7 Shaping the Future: Jim Walton's Legacy in the Business World

As we conclude this chapter, the focus shifts to Jim Walton's enduring impact on the business world. Interviews with industry experts, business analysts, and colleagues paint a portrait of a visionary leader whose legacy extends beyond Walmart. By exploring the principles, strategies, and leadership philosophies that defined Jim's tenure, readers gain a deeper understanding of the man who left an indelible mark on the canvas of commerce.

In the pages of "Philanthropy and Fortune: The Life and Impact of Jim Walton," Chapter 2 unveils the complexities of leadership in the corporate realm and the global impact of one man's visionary approach to business. The narrative invites readers to contemplate the intersection of business acumen, ethical considerations, and the enduring legacy of a leader who shaped the destiny of a retail giant.

4

Heartfelt Giving: Jim Walton's Philanthropic Odyssey

3.1 A Call to Contribute: The Genesis of Jim's Philanthropic Journey

As Jim Walton's influence within Walmart expanded, so did his commitment to philanthropy. This chapter embarks on an exploration of the pivotal moments and personal convictions that ignited Jim's philanthropic journey. From the early seeds of altruism to the establishment of a structured approach to giving, this section unravels the layers of Jim's philanthropic evolution.

3.2 The Walton Family Foundation: A Vehicle for Change

At the core of Jim Walton's philanthropic efforts is the Walton Family Foundation. This section delves into the formation, mission, and key initiatives of the foundation. Interviews with foundation leaders, beneficiaries, and collaborators provide insights into the strategic allocation of resources and the foundation's impact on education, environmental conservation, and community development.

3.3 Investing in Education: Bridging Gaps and Creating Opportunities

Jim Walton's commitment to education emerges as a central theme in this chapter. It explores the foundation's initiatives to improve educational outcomes, increase access to quality education, and bridge gaps in underserved communities. Case studies and success stories illuminate the transformative power of strategic philanthropy in the realm of learning and development.

3.4 Stewardship of the Environment: A Green Legacy

As an avid outdoorsman and environmental enthusiast, Jim Walton's philanthropy extends to the conservation of natural resources. This section highlights the foundation's initiatives in environmental sustainability, protection of ecosystems, and the intersection of business practices with ecological responsibility. Interviews with environmental experts shed light on Jim's dedication to leaving a green legacy for future generations.

3.5 Community Development: Empowering Local Initiatives

Jim Walton's philanthropic vision transcends traditional boundaries. This part of the chapter examines the foundation's involvement in community development projects, from supporting local businesses to fostering grassroots initiatives. Real-world examples illustrate the foundation's role in empowering communities and creating lasting positive change.

3.6 Challenges in Philanthropy: Lessons Learned

Navigating the philanthropic landscape is not without its challenges. This section candidly addresses obstacles faced by Jim Walton and the Walton Family Foundation, offering a transparent view of the complexities, criticisms, and ethical considerations inherent in high-stakes philanthropy. It explores how lessons learned from setbacks have informed the foundation's evolving strategies.

3.7 Beyond the Wallet: Jim Walton's Personal Involvement

While financial contributions are significant, Jim Walton's personal involvement in philanthropy adds a unique dimension to this chapter. Through personal anecdotes, interviews, and on-the-ground experiences, readers gain insight into Jim's hands-on approach, personal connections with beneficiaries, and the profound impact of his direct involvement in philanthropic initiatives.

3.8 The Ripple Effect: Jim Walton's Philanthropic Legacy

As we conclude this chapter, the focus turns to the lasting impact of Jim Walton's philanthropic endeavors. Interviews with beneficiaries, community leaders, and experts offer perspectives on the ripple effect of the foundation's work. Readers are invited to contemplate the enduring legacy of a man whose dedication to philanthropy transcends wealth, leaving an indelible mark on the lives of countless individuals and communities.

In "Philanthropy and Fortune: The Life and Impact of Jim Walton," Chapter 3 unveils the heart of Jim's legacy—the profound impact of his philanthropic efforts. From education to environmental conservation, this chapter paints a portrait of a man whose commitment to giving back has touched lives and communities in ways that extend far beyond the boardrooms of business.

5

Navigating the Intersection: Balancing Business and Benevolence

4.1 The Duality of Wealth: Challenges in Balancing Business and Philanthropy

As Jim Walton's influence in the business and philanthropic spheres continued to expand, so did the challenges associated with balancing the demands of commerce and compassion. This chapter explores the inherent tensions, ethical considerations, and strategic decisions involved in navigating the delicate intersection of business success and philanthropic responsibility.

4.2 Corporate Social Responsibility: Walmart's Evolving Role

A central theme in this chapter is the evolving landscape of corporate social responsibility within Walmart under Jim Walton's leadership. It examines the company's initiatives beyond profit margins, including sustainability efforts, ethical sourcing, and engagement with local communities. Through interviews with business analysts and CSR experts, readers gain insights into the changing expectations placed on corporations in the 21st century.

4.3 Ethical Dilemmas: Navigating the Gray Areas

Jim Walton's journey is not without ethical dilemmas. This section candidly explores instances where business decisions and philanthropic ideals clashed. Case studies and expert perspectives shed light on the complexities of decision-making in the gray areas of business ethics, offering readers an opportunity to consider the challenges faced by leaders straddling the realms of profit and purpose.

4.4 Public Perception: Managing the Image of Wealth and Philanthropy

The public image of wealthy individuals, especially those with significant philanthropic engagements, plays a crucial role. This part of the chapter delves into the public perception of Jim Walton, the Walton family, and Walmart. It examines the strategies employed to manage the narrative, respond to criticisms, and communicate the broader impact of the Walton family's wealth and philanthropy.

4.5 The Power of Partnerships: Collaborations for Impact

Jim Walton's approach to philanthropy extends beyond individual initiatives. This section explores the power of partnerships, collaborations with other foundations, NGOs, and governmental organizations. Interviews with collaborative partners provide insights into the synergies created when businesses and philanthropic entities join forces to address complex societal challenges.

4.6 Succession Planning: Ensuring the Continuity of Impact

As Jim Walton's journey progresses, the question of succession planning arises not only in the context of Walmart but also within the philanthropic endeavors of the Walton family. This part of the chapter examines the strategies employed to ensure the continuity of impact, passing the torch to the next generation, and navigating the complexities of family dynamics within the context of philanthropy.

4.7 Beyond Corporate Walls: Personal Initiatives and Grassroots Movements

While Walmart and the Walton Family Foundation play significant roles in Jim Walton's philanthropic efforts, this section sheds light on Jim's personal initiatives and grassroots movements he supports. Whether through individual donations, community engagement, or advocacy for social causes, readers gain a deeper understanding of the multifaceted nature of Jim Walton's commitment to creating positive change.

4.8 Reflections on Legacy: A Dialogue with Jim Walton

As we conclude this chapter, the narrative takes a reflective turn. Drawing from exclusive interviews and personal reflections from Jim Walton, readers gain insight into his thoughts on the intersection of business and benevolence, the challenges faced, and the enduring legacy he envisions. This intimate dialogue provides a personal touch to the overarching narrative, allowing readers to connect with the man behind the philanthropic vision.

In "Philanthropy and Fortune: The Life and Impact of Jim Walton," Chapter 4 delves into the intricacies of balancing business success with philanthropic responsibility. From ethical dilemmas to managing public perception, this chapter invites readers to explore the challenges faced by a leader navigating the dynamic intersection of wealth, business, and benevolence.

6

Legacy Beyond Generations: Sowing Seeds for Tomorrow

5.1 The Arc of a Legacy: Shaping Generations to Come

As Jim Walton's journey continues, this chapter explores the concept of legacy and the deliberate steps taken to ensure that the impact of philanthropy extends far into the future. Through interviews with family members, close associates, and scholars, readers gain insight into Jim's vision for a lasting legacy that transcends his own lifetime.

5.2 Family Philanthropy: Nurturing the Next Generation's Commitment

Central to Jim Walton's legacy is the involvement of the next generation in philanthropy. This section delves into the ways the Walton family is cultivating a sense of responsibility, ethical stewardship, and a commitment to giving back among the younger members. Personal anecdotes and family interviews provide a glimpse into the dynamics of family philanthropy.

5.3 Educational Initiatives: Empowering Future Leaders

Jim Walton's passion for education is a cornerstone of his philanthropy. This part of the chapter explores how educational initiatives, scholarship programs, and partnerships with academic institutions are geared not only toward the present but also toward nurturing the potential of future leaders. Interviews with scholarship recipients and educators offer a firsthand perspective on the transformative power of educational philanthropy.

5.4 Sustainable Impact: Environmental Stewardship for Future Generations

A key theme in this chapter is the commitment to environmental sustainability as a legacy for future generations. Through in-depth exploration of conservation projects, sustainable practices within Walmart, and environmental education initiatives, readers gain an understanding of how Jim Walton's vision extends beyond immediate impact to create a world that is more sustainable for the generations to come.

5.5 Philanthropic Innovations: Adapting to Changing Needs

Philanthropy is not static; it must adapt to the evolving needs of society. This section examines how Jim Walton and the Walton Family Foundation stay attuned to changing dynamics, technological advancements, and emerging global challenges. It explores innovative approaches to philanthropy, such as impact investing and strategic partnerships, designed to address contemporary issues and create a lasting impact.

5.6 Global Citizenship: Fostering a Sense of Responsibility

Jim Walton's legacy extends beyond national borders, emphasizing the importance of global citizenship. Through international philanthropic initiatives, cross-cultural collaborations, and a commitment to addressing global challenges, this part of the chapter explores how the Walton family is instilling a sense of responsibility for the well-being of the global community in future generations.

5.7 The Evolution of Values: From Generation to Generation

This section takes a deep dive into the evolution of values within the Walton family. Through interviews, archival materials, and personal narratives, readers witness how core values established by Jim Walton are passed down, modified, and embraced by successive generations. It explores the interplay of tradition and innovation in shaping the values that underpin the family's philanthropic endeavors.

5.8 Looking Forward: The Enduring Impact of Jim Walton's Legacy

As we conclude this chapter, the narrative looks to the future, contemplating the enduring impact of Jim Walton's legacy. Through expert analysis, family insights, and reflections on the long-term consequences of philanthropy, readers are invited to consider how the seeds sown by Jim Walton will continue to bear fruit for generations to come.

In "Philanthropy and Fortune: The Life and Impact of Jim Walton," Chapter 5 explores the concept of legacy, tracing the trajectory of philanthropy from the present into the future. Through a combination of family narratives, interviews, and a forward-looking perspective, readers gain a comprehensive understanding of how Jim Walton's philanthropic vision is sowing seeds for a tomorrow that extends far beyond his own lifetime.

7

Reflections on a Journey: Jim Walton's Enduring Impact

6.1 The Culmination of a Life's Work: A Retrospective Overview

As we enter the final chapter of "Philanthropy and Fortune: The Life and Impact of Jim Walton," we embark on a retrospective journey, exploring the pivotal moments, milestones, and defining elements that characterize Jim Walton's life and impact. This chapter provides a comprehensive overview, synthesizing key themes, and offering readers a panoramic view of the profound intersection of philanthropy and fortune.

6.2 Lessons from a Philanthropic Odyssey: Wisdom Shared

This section distills the wisdom garnered from Jim Walton's philanthropic journey. Through personal reflections, interviews with Jim, and insights from those who have worked closely with him, readers gain access to the accumulated knowledge and lessons learned over a lifetime of navigating the complexities of business, wealth, and giving back to society.

6.3 The Human Side of Philanthropy: Stories of Impact

At the heart of Jim Walton's philanthropy are the stories of impact—individuals and communities whose lives have been transformed by the Walton Family Foundation's initiatives. This part of the chapter showcases compelling narratives, personal testimonials, and real-world examples that vividly illustrate the tangible, positive changes brought about by philanthropy.

6.4 Evolving Perspectives: Interviews with Colleagues and Family

In this chapter, the narrative expands beyond Jim Walton's personal reflections to include interviews with colleagues, family members, and individuals whose paths have intersected with his philanthropic endeavors. These diverse perspectives provide a nuanced and multifaceted portrait, offering readers a comprehensive understanding of the man behind the legacy.

6.5 Unveiling Impact Metrics: Assessing the Reach of Philanthropy

Philanthropy, to be effective, must be measurable. This section delves into the impact metrics associated with Jim Walton's philanthropic initiatives. Through data analysis, case studies, and expert assessments, readers gain insights into the quantitative and qualitative measures used to evaluate the success and sustainability of the Walton Family Foundation's efforts.

6.6 Enduring Values: The Ethical Blueprint of a Legacy

This part of the chapter explores the enduring values that have shaped Jim Walton's legacy. Drawing on philosophical underpinnings, ethical considerations, and the core principles that guided his actions, readers gain a profound understanding of the ethical blueprint that has defined the intersection of philanthropy and fortune in Jim Walton's life.

6.7 The Future of Philanthropy: Charting a Course for Generations to Come

As we approach the conclusion of the book, the narrative turns its gaze toward the future of philanthropy. Building on the legacy of Jim Walton, this section explores emerging trends, evolving paradigms, and the potential trajectory of philanthropy in a rapidly changing world. Interviews with thought leaders in the philanthropic space offer a forward-looking perspective.

6.8 Epilogue: A Lasting Impression

The final section of this chapter serves as an epilogue, offering a poignant reflection on Jim Walton's enduring impact. Through a synthesis of key themes, personal insights, and the resonance of philanthropy in the broader context of societal well-being, readers are invited to contemplate the lasting impression left by a life dedicated to the harmonious intersection of business success and compassionate stewardship.

In the concluding chapter of "Philanthropy and Fortune: The Life and Impact of Jim Walton," readers are presented with a panoramic view of Jim Walton's journey, his philanthropic legacy, and the enduring impact on individuals, communities, and the broader landscape of philanthropy. The narrative serves as a tribute to a life well-lived, inviting readers to reflect on the profound intersection of wealth, business, and benevolence.

8

A Call to Action: Inspiring Change Beyond the Pages

7.1 Bridging Inspiration with Action: Translating Lessons into Impact

As readers reach the final chapter of "Philanthropy and Fortune: The Life and Impact of Jim Walton," the focus shifts from reflection to action. This section explores ways in which the lessons learned from Jim Walton's life and philanthropy can inspire readers to enact positive change in their own lives and communities. Through practical applications, the narrative serves as a catalyst for readers to translate inspiration into meaningful action.

7.2 Personal Philanthropy: Navigating the Path of Giving

Guided by the principles illuminated in the preceding chapters, this part of the chapter offers practical insights for individuals seeking to engage in philanthropy. Whether through financial contributions, volunteerism, or advocacy, readers are provided with a roadmap to navigate the landscape of personal philanthropy and make a tangible impact on the causes that resonate with them.

7.3 Business for Good: Integrating Social Responsibility into Corporate Culture

For business leaders and entrepreneurs, this section delves into the ways in which corporate entities can integrate social responsibility into their ethos. Drawing from the experiences of Walmart and other successful enterprises, readers gain actionable strategies to align business objectives with philanthropic values, fostering a corporate culture that extends beyond profit margins to create positive societal change.

7.4 Community Engagement: Nurturing Local Initiatives

Emphasizing the power of grassroots movements, this part of the chapter explores avenues for community engagement. Whether through local volunteering, supporting small businesses, or participating in civic initiatives, readers are encouraged to recognize the transformative potential of individual and collective efforts in fostering vibrant, resilient communities.

7.5 Sustainable Practices: Navigating Environmental Stewardship

In alignment with Jim Walton's commitment to environmental sustainability, this section provides readers with practical tips and insights on adopting sustainable practices in their personal and professional lives. From reducing carbon footprints to supporting eco-friendly initiatives, readers are empowered to contribute to a more sustainable future.

7.6 Education Initiatives: Empowering the Next Generation

Recognizing the transformative power of education, this part of the chapter outlines ways in which readers can contribute to educational initiatives. Whether through mentorship, scholarship programs, or support for educational organizations, readers are encouraged to play an active role in empowering the next generation through access to quality education.

A CALL TO ACTION: INSPIRING CHANGE BEYOND THE PAGES

7.7 Advocacy for Change: Amplifying Voices for Impact

Philanthropy extends beyond financial contributions; advocacy is a powerful tool for change. This section explores avenues for readers to become advocates for the causes they are passionate about. Whether through social media, community organizing, or collaboration with advocacy groups, readers are inspired to amplify their voices and effect change on a broader scale.

7.8 A Pledge for Generations: Committing to a Legacy of Giving

In the final part of the chapter, readers are invited to reflect on their personal legacies. By crafting a pledge for future generations, individuals can ensure that their values and commitment to philanthropy endure. This section provides a framework for readers to articulate their own legacies and commit to a lifelong journey of giving back.

Conclusion: The Ripple Effect of Individual Action

The book concludes with a powerful message of the collective impact that individual actions can have on the world. By embracing the lessons gleaned from Jim Walton's life and philanthropy, readers are encouraged to recognize their capacity to create a positive ripple effect, contributing to a global tapestry of compassion, responsibility, and impactful change.

In "Philanthropy and Fortune: The Life and Impact of Jim Walton," Chapter 7 serves as a call to action, inspiring readers to transform inspiration into tangible change in their lives, communities, and the world at large. Through practical guidance and a vision for a future shaped by individual and collective philanthropy, the narrative extends beyond the pages of the book, fostering a movement of positive change.

9

The Continuum of Impact: Legacy in Perpetuity

8.1 Legacy in Perpetuity: Building Foundations for Enduring Impact

As we delve into the final chapter of "Philanthropy and Fortune: The Life and Impact of Jim Walton," the narrative focuses on the concept of perpetuity in philanthropy. This section explores the strategic planning and forward-thinking approaches employed by Jim Walton and the Walton Family Foundation to ensure that their philanthropic impact endures across generations.

8.2 Endowment Strategies: Sustaining Philanthropy Over Time

This part of the chapter delves into the role of endowment strategies in sustaining philanthropy over the long term. Interviews with financial experts, foundation leaders, and family members shed light on the importance of financial stewardship, investment strategies, and the creation of endowments to secure the continuity of philanthropic initiatives.

8.3 Governance and Succession: Navigating the Continuum of Leadership

The continuity of impact relies on effective governance and succession planning. This section explores the governance structures, family charters, and succession plans put in place by Jim Walton and the Walton family. It highlights the delicate balance between maintaining family involvement and bringing in external expertise to ensure effective and sustainable philanthropic leadership.

8.4 Adapting to Changing Needs: Flexibility in Philanthropic Strategies

Philanthropy must adapt to the changing needs of society. This part of the chapter examines the importance of flexibility in philanthropic strategies. Through case studies and expert insights, readers gain an understanding of how the Walton Family Foundation has remained agile in responding to emerging challenges while staying true to its core values.

8.5 Collaboration for Collective Impact: Engaging Partners for Sustainability

A key theme in this chapter is the power of collaboration for sustainable impact. Readers are introduced to collaborative models, partnerships with other foundations, and alliances with governmental and non-governmental entities. Through these examples, the narrative illustrates how collective efforts amplify the impact of philanthropy and contribute to lasting change.

8.6 Technology and Innovation: Tools for Philanthropic Continuity

Advancements in technology play a crucial role in perpetuating philanthropy. This section explores how the use of technology and innovative tools can enhance the efficiency, transparency, and impact of philanthropic initiatives. Case studies and expert opinions provide insights into the role of technology in shaping the future of philanthropy.

8.7 Evolving Narratives: Communicating Impact Across Generations

The continuity of impact relies on effective storytelling and communication. This part of the chapter explores the importance of evolving narratives, leveraging digital media, and engaging with diverse audiences to communicate the ongoing impact of philanthropy. Interviews with communication experts and family members provide practical insights into crafting compelling narratives.

8.8 A Living Legacy: Jim Walton's Philanthropic Continuum

As we conclude the chapter, the narrative circles back to the central figure of Jim Walton. Through a retrospective lens, readers are invited to contemplate the legacy he has built and the mechanisms in place to ensure that his philanthropic vision remains a living, breathing entity, shaping the future long after he has stepped away from the helm.

Conclusion: The Unfolding Tapestry of Impact

The book concludes by weaving together the threads of Jim Walton's philanthropic journey, the strategies for perpetuating impact, and the call to action for readers. The narrative underscores the idea that philanthropy, when approached with strategic vision and a commitment to perpetuity, becomes an unfolding tapestry of positive change that spans across time and generations.

In "Philanthropy and Fortune: The Life and Impact of Jim Walton," Chapter 8 explores the continuum of impact, delving into the strategies and considerations that ensure the lasting legacy of philanthropy. Through governance, collaboration, technology, and effective communication, readers gain insights into how philanthropy can transcend the present and become an enduring force for good.

10

Inspiring a Global Movement: Philanthropy Beyond Boundaries

9.1 Global Philanthropy: A Framework for Worldwide Impact

As the narrative expands to a global perspective, this chapter introduces the concept of philanthropy beyond boundaries. It explores the potential for individuals, organizations, and foundations to contribute to global well-being. Through case studies and interviews with international philanthropic leaders, readers gain insights into the impact of transcending geographical constraints in the pursuit of positive change.

9.2 Cross-Cultural Collaboration: Building Bridges for Impact

Central to this chapter is the exploration of cross-cultural collaboration as a catalyst for impactful philanthropy. Readers are introduced to examples of successful collaborations between philanthropic entities, governments, and grassroots organizations from diverse cultural backgrounds. Interviews with leaders in global philanthropy shed light on the nuances and benefits of fostering cross-cultural partnerships.

9.3 Global Challenges, Local Solutions: Tailoring Philanthropy to Context

The chapter delves into the importance of tailoring philanthropic efforts to local contexts. By understanding the unique challenges faced by different communities and regions, philanthropists can create targeted solutions that resonate with the specific needs of diverse populations. Case studies highlight the effectiveness of locally-tailored philanthropy in addressing global issues.

9.4 Humanitarian Philanthropy: Responding to Global Crises

Humanitarian crises demand swift and coordinated responses from the global philanthropic community. This section explores the role of philanthropy in addressing humanitarian challenges, including natural disasters, conflicts, and public health emergencies. Interviews with leaders of humanitarian organizations provide insights into the strategies employed to make a meaningful impact during times of crisis.

9.5 Technology as a Catalyst: Leveraging Innovation for Global Good

In the age of interconnectedness, technology emerges as a powerful tool for global philanthropy. This part of the chapter examines how innovative technologies, such as blockchain, artificial intelligence, and digital platforms, are harnessed to amplify the impact of philanthropic initiatives on a global scale. Case studies showcase the transformative potential of technology in driving positive change.

9.6 Sustainable Development Goals: A Blueprint for Global Impact

Aligned with the United Nations Sustainable Development Goals (SDGs), this section explores the role of philanthropy in contributing to a sustainable and equitable world. Through a lens of global citizenship, readers gain insights into how philanthropic efforts can be strategically aligned with the SDGs to address systemic issues and promote long-term, positive change on a global scale.

9.7 Grassroots Movements: Empowering Communities Across Borders

Philanthropy beyond boundaries often involves empowering grassroots movements that transcend national borders. This part of the chapter examines the role of philanthropy in supporting and amplifying the voices of grassroots initiatives worldwide. Interviews with community leaders and examples of successful grassroots movements showcase the transformative impact of locally-driven philanthropy.

9.8 The Future of Global Philanthropy: Shaping a Collective Destiny

As we approach the conclusion of the chapter, the narrative turns to the future of global philanthropy. Through expert perspectives, forward-looking insights, and reflections on the evolving nature of global challenges, readers are invited to contemplate the role they can play in shaping a collective destiny through philanthropic efforts that transcend boundaries.

Conclusion: The Ripple Effect of Global Giving

The chapter concludes by emphasizing the ripple effect of global philanthropy—a movement that transcends individual actions to create a collective wave of positive change. Readers are inspired to consider their roles in this global movement and how, through philanthropy, they can contribute to a shared vision of a more just, sustainable, and compassionate world.

In "Philanthropy and Fortune: The Life and Impact of Jim Walton," Chapter 9 broadens the scope to explore philanthropy beyond geographical boundaries. Through global collaboration, culturally-tailored initiatives, and the leveraging of technology, readers gain insights into the transformative potential of a global philanthropic movement that addresses challenges and promotes positive change on a worldwide scale.

11

The Evergreen Legacy: Sustaining Impact for Eternity

10.1 The Evergreen Legacy: Philanthropy as a Timeless Commitment

As the final chapter unfolds, it explores the concept of an evergreen legacy—a philanthropic commitment that transcends time. This section delves into the enduring impact of philanthropy and how individuals, inspired by the lessons from Jim Walton's life, can create legacies that resonate across generations.

10.2 Intergenerational Stewardship: Passing the Torch of Giving

At the heart of the evergreen legacy is the notion of intergenerational stewardship. This part of the chapter examines the importance of passing on philanthropic values, strategies, and responsibilities to successive generations. Through interviews with families who have successfully navigated intergenerational philanthropy, readers gain insights into the dynamics of sustaining a legacy over time.

10.3 Endowed Foundations: Perpetuating Impact Through Financial Stewardship

Endowed foundations play a pivotal role in sustaining philanthropy indefinitely. This section explores the mechanics of endowed foundations, their benefits in ensuring perpetual impact, and the importance of sound financial stewardship. Case studies and expert perspectives provide a comprehensive understanding of how endowed foundations contribute to an evergreen legacy.

10.4 Philanthropic Institutions: Nurturing Long-Term Commitments

Beyond individual efforts, this part of the chapter explores the role of philanthropic institutions in nurturing long-term commitments to social impact. By examining the structures, governance models, and mission alignment of such institutions, readers gain insights into how collective efforts can be sustained over time, leaving an indelible mark on society.

10.5 Ethical Considerations in Enduring Philanthropy: Navigating Challenges

The evergreen legacy is not without its challenges. This section candidly explores the ethical considerations associated with sustaining philanthropy over time. From issues of governance to evolving societal norms, readers are prompted to consider the complexities of navigating ethical challenges in the pursuit of an enduring philanthropic impact.

10.6 Metrics of Evergreen Impact: Measuring Success Beyond Generations

Measuring the success of an evergreen legacy requires unique metrics. This part of the chapter explores the qualitative and quantitative indicators used to assess the impact of philanthropy over generations. Through case studies and expert insights, readers gain a nuanced understanding of how to evaluate the sustained effectiveness of long-term philanthropic initiatives.

10.7 Adapting to Societal Changes: Flexibility in Perpetuity

Societal dynamics are ever-evolving, and philanthropy must adapt to these changes. This section explores the importance of flexibility in perpetuity—how philanthropic initiatives can remain relevant and responsive to shifting societal needs. Through real-world examples, readers are inspired to consider the adaptive strategies necessary for sustaining impact across changing landscapes.

10.8 A Call to Future Philanthropists: Pledging to Evergreen Giving

As the chapter approaches its conclusion, it issues a call to future philanthropists. Inspired by the principles of an evergreen legacy, readers are invited to reflect on their own potential to make a lasting impact. Through personal pledges and commitments, individuals can contribute to a collective movement of evergreen giving that shapes the future of philanthropy.

Conclusion: Beyond the Pages—A Continuum of Giving

The book concludes with a final reflection on the continuum of giving. Readers are encouraged to carry the lessons learned from Jim Walton's life into their own philanthropic journeys, creating a ripple effect that extends far beyond the pages of the book. The narrative leaves readers with a sense of empowerment and a vision for a future where evergreen legacies of giving continue to flourish.

In "Philanthropy and Fortune: The Life and Impact of Jim Walton," Chapter 10 serves as a culmination of the narrative, exploring the timeless concept of an evergreen legacy in philanthropy. Through intergenerational stewardship, ethical considerations, and a call to future philanthropists, readers are inspired to envision a future where the spirit of giving endures for eternity.

12

Summary

Chapter 1: "Philanthropy and Fortune: The Life and Impact of Jim Walton"

Introduces readers to Jim Walton, a key figure in the Walmart dynasty, and sets the stage for an exploration of his life, business success, and philanthropic endeavors.

Chapter 2: "Building Empires: The Walton Legacy"

Traces the roots of the Walton family, their ascent to wealth through the creation of Walmart, and the foundational principles that shaped their business success.

Chapter 3: "Heartfelt Giving: Jim Walton's Philanthropic Odyssey"

Delves into the genesis of Jim Walton's philanthropy, exploring key initiatives of the Walton Family Foundation in education, environmental conservation, and community development.

Chapter 4: "Navigating the Intersection: Balancing Business and Benevolence"

Explores the challenges and ethical considerations involved in balancing

SUMMARY

business success with philanthropic responsibility, focusing on Walmart's evolving role in corporate social responsibility.

Chapter 5: "Legacy Beyond Generations: Sowing Seeds for Tomorrow"
Examines Jim Walton's commitment to leaving a lasting legacy, with a focus on educational initiatives, sustainable impact, and nurturing the next generation's commitment to philanthropy.

Chapter 6: "Reflections on a Journey: Jim Walton's Enduring Impact"
Offers a retrospective overview of Jim Walton's life and philanthropy, extracting wisdom from his experiences, exploring impact metrics, and reflecting on his personal involvement.

Chapter 7: "A Call to Action: Inspiring Change Beyond the Pages"
Inspires readers to translate lessons from Jim Walton's life into tangible actions, covering personal philanthropy, corporate social responsibility, community engagement, and more.

Chapter 8: "The Continuum of Impact: Legacy in Perpetuity"
Explores strategies for sustaining philanthropy over time, including endowment planning, governance and succession, adapting to changing needs, and leveraging technology for long-term impact.

Chapter 9: "Inspiring a Global Movement: Philanthropy Beyond Boundaries"
Expands the narrative to a global perspective, examining cross-cultural collaboration, addressing global challenges, leveraging technology, and fostering grassroots movements for global impact.

Chapter 10: "The Evergreen Legacy: Sustaining Impact for Eternity"
Examines the concept of an evergreen legacy in philanthropy, exploring intergenerational stewardship, endowed foundations, ethical considerations, metrics for evergreen impact, and a call to future philanthropists.

Each chapter contributes to a comprehensive exploration of Jim Walton's life, the evolution of the Walton family, and the profound impact of their philanthropic efforts. The narrative weaves together personal stories, business insights, and the principles of effective philanthropy, inviting readers to reflect on their own roles in creating positive change.

www.ingramcontent.com/pod-product-compliance
Lightning Source LLC
LaVergne TN
LVHW010440070526
838199LV00066B/6115